IMAGINATION ON DISPLAY

FROM CAVES TO YOUR COMPUTER   A NEW WAY OF SEEING THE WORLD

WRITTEN AND ILLUSTRATED BY ALEXANDER MOSCATTINI

Contents

From the Caves to Computers

Introduction

The story of painting and image-making covers mans activity from painting on cave walls to modern times where the computer has become the dominant tool when it comes to creating images. Most books on this topic will usually have hundreds of pages devoted mostly to lengthy description about the period or artists and the reading is very academic in nature geared more to the serious art historian. This book attempt to put the subject of art history in more simple, fun and palatable terms that may be enjoyed by everyone who has ever wonder what all the fuss is about certain paintings, and why there are people who are willing to pay millions of dollars for an image painted on canvas by a particular artist like Picasso or van Gogh. In this book the importance of each art movement or period is described in simple terms which focus on the main contribution to the advancement of the way we see the world and of human cognitive abilities. A list of artists names are provided on each page if the reader wishes to further research the people who made and contributed to the style and movement.

Cave Paintings

Around 30,000 years ago our ancestors became the first species to try and reproduce an image of something they saw. No other species before or after has ever accomplished this task. Creating or reproducing images is probably one of the first great advancements that humans had made which put them at a higher intellectual level compared to all other creatures.

Check out: the Lascaux Caves and Chauvet Caves in France.

Mesopotamia and the Middle East

From Mesopotamian an ancient country (which existed approximately 3500 - 2000 B.C.) in south west Asia, between the Tigris and Euphrates rivers, people there for the first time started to create human figures out of stone, clay and other materials. Later, in the ancient cities of Akkad approximately 2300 B.C. and Assyria approximately 1000 B.C. we find people creating human figures with wings and other animalistic features.

Egyptian Hieroglyphics

During the period of ancient Egypt (approximately from 3000 B.C. - 50 B.C.), we see for the first time a civilization trying to reproduce images in order to convey ideas and beliefs using symbols (know as hieroglyphics) carved or painted onto a wall of tombs found in pyramids. Statues of Pharaohs (kings and queens) appear stiff in profile with a proportional frontal direction appearance.

Key example: Tomb of Horemheb, c. 1350 B.C. Egyptian Museum, Cairo

Greek Art

The Golden age of Greek art took place approximately from 1100 B.C. - 500 B.C. During this time artists started to show the ideal man and woman with their muscular bodies and possible emotions. Movement of the human figure takes on an important role during this era. Also, the paintings show landscapes. Greeks used these images to decorate vases and jewelry.

Key examples: 5th century Greek Pottery.

Roman Art

An important new advancement in art took place (approximately from 200 B.C - 200 A.D.) with Roman art. We find images of natural looking men and women placed in story-line or narrative scenes. These scenes tell of certain events that took place. The events of a conquest could be depicted in mosaic form covering a large wall. Landscape paintings showed exceptional detail and realism.

Key example: Ara Pacis Augustas (Altar of the Augustan Peace).

Medieval Art

We find that Medieval Art took place approximately from 730 A.D. to 1450 A.D. and centered on the city of Constantinople (today known as Istanbul Turkey). Artists adopted styles from the Roman Empire and created monumental frescos and mosaics of Icons inside churches.

Key Artists: Cimabue, Paolo Veneziano, and Theophanes the Greek.

Gothic Art

Gothic Art started in 1140 with the use of human figures as columns on a church in France. Gothic paintings followed with images that were more somber, dark and expressed more emotions than previous periods. Gothic Art can be found in England, France, Germany and Italy. It is important to note that during this period artists started to sign their names to their work. Gothic Art was a dominant force until the Renaissance period which began in the early 1450's.

Key Artist: Simone Martini

Renaissance Art

The Renaissance (rebirth) took place from 1450's to 1700's. The movement tried to revive the past learning's of the ancient Greeks and Romans. There was a new sense of trying to produce the beauty of nature. In Northern Italy, painters like Leonardo Da Vinci developed new techniques studying light, shadow, perspective and human anatomy. It is important to note that during this time in the Netherlands an artist named Jan Van Eyck invented oil paint to be applied on canvas. Many artists began to depict themes of everyday life.

Key Artists: Sandro Botticelli, Michelangeloi, Raphael and Leonardo da Vinci. Giorgione, Titian ,Giovanni Bellini Albrecht Dürer, Hieronymus Bosch and Pieter Bruegel.

Impressionism

During the Impressionistic movement centered in France from the 1860's to 1880's. Artists for the first time used strong, bright unmixed colors applied in small dabs on a canvas to create the impression of natural reflected light. These artists were trying to create images without using lines, applying only color.

Key Artists: Claude Monet, Alfred Sisley Pierre-Auguste Renoir. Camille Pissarro, Frederic Bazille, Edgar Degas, Gustave Caillebotte, Edouard Manet, .

Post Impressionism Art

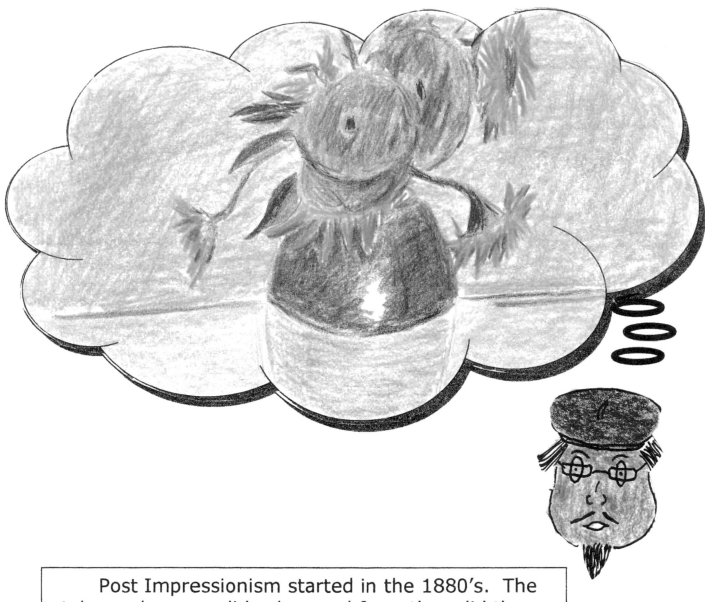

Post Impressionism started in the 1880's. The style used more solid colors and form than did the Impressionists. The Post Impressionists incorporated structure and form in their work and were looking to bring a sense of emotion in their work.

Key Artistes: Paul Gauguin, Paul Cézanne, Vincent van Gogh, Henri Rousseau and Henri de Toulouse-Lautrec.

Fauvism

At an art show in Paris in 1905, a group of artist shocked the art world by showing their work which used bold, brilliant color applied to subject matter that appeared flat. The style was more primitive and less naturalistic than the artist were capable of producing at the time because of this an art critic called the painters "Les Fauves" or "Wild Beasts".

Key Artists: Albert Marquet, Andre Derain, Maurice de Vlaminck and Henri Matisse.

12

Futurism

The Futurism movement started around 1907 as a rebellion against the worshiping of the Old Masters and religion. Futurists embraced technology, along with the love of speed and violence. Inspired by photography, the Futurists took movement and broke it down into small sequences. They used repetition of line to create rhythm on canvases.

Key Artists: Filippo Tommaso Marinetti, Umberto Boccioni, Giacomo Balla, Carlo Carrà, and Gino Severini.

13

Cubism

Cubism as a movement started around 1910. In the works of artists like Picasso, we see for the first time someone looking at an object from different perspectives (i.e. front view and side view) and trying to reproduce an image using both views simultaneously.

Key Artists: Georges Braque , Pablo Picasso, and Paul Cezanne.

14

Dada

Dada was a movement that took hold from 1916 to 1924. After World War I, some artists became cynical of humanity and tried to create images of a world turned up side down. Previous artists were concerned with sensibility and beauty, the Dadaist tried to offend. Dada was a movement against art that became art.

Key Artists: Jean Arp, Francis Picabia and Marcel Duchamp

De Stijl

This style of art started around 1920. In order to develop a new style, artists (around Holland) began to create a non-objective type of art movement. They used primary colors to create a balance structure within lines and rectangles.

Key Artist: Piet Mondrian,

Surrealism

Surrealism as a movement started around 1920. For the first time, artists tried to portray the subconscious mind using different fantastical visual images that seem to come from dreams. Surrealist, as these artist were called, tried to distort their subject matter to the point were the objects had no normal logical function.

Key Artists: Max Ernst, Giorgio de Chirico, Man Ray, Joan Miro, Rene Magritte, and Salvador Dali.

Regional Art
Group of Seven

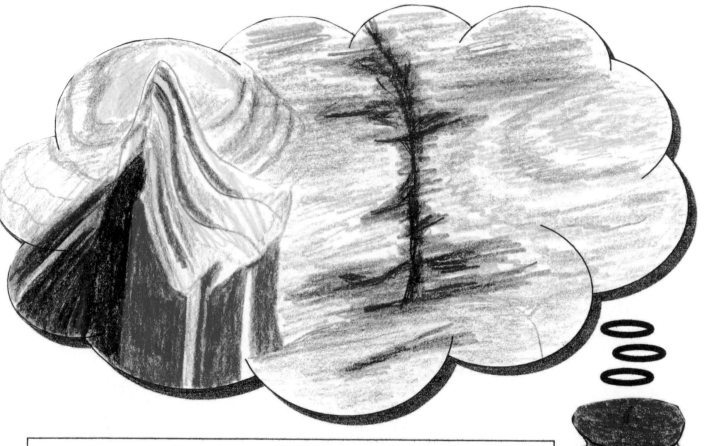

Influence by other styles like Impressionism, a group of artists in Canada saw nature as a powerful force which they believed people cannot easily refine, control, or improve. These artist presented nature as a more abstract powerful force shaping the character of a country and its people. In Canada these artists became known as the Group of Seven. Like Canada if we look around the world we find regional artists everywhere trying to capture the beauty and the essence of the land where they live.

Key Artists: Franklin Carmichael, A.J. Casson, Lionel Fitzgerald, Arthur Lismer, Lawren Harris, Edwin Holgate, A.Y. Jackson, J.E.H. MacDonald, F.H. Varley. Along with Tom Thomson and Emily Carr.

Cartoons

As early as 1070's we can find cartoon like images in art. If one looks at what is known as The Bayeux Tapestry, we find cartoon like images of men in battle depicting the Norman invasion of England. Cartoons became very popular during the 1920's and since then Illustrations have personified not only human's images but also everything from mice, ducks to objects like cups, cars and candle sticks.

Key example: The Bayeux Tapestry

Cartoons and Animation

With the advent of animation as in talking movies, we see the images of cartoon characters like a mouse or duck as having human personalities and capabilities. The use of images expands into the realm of entertainment.

Key example: Walt Disney

Pop Art

This movement started around 1950. For the first time, Artists came to use advertising art, comic strips, and other commonplace objects (i.e. soap boxes or soup cans) as the subject they used for their paintings and sculptures. Artists declare that common everyday packaging of goods and images of celebrities are something that they can use as their subject matter for their creations.

Key Artists: Andy Warhol and Roy Lichtenstein.

Expressionism

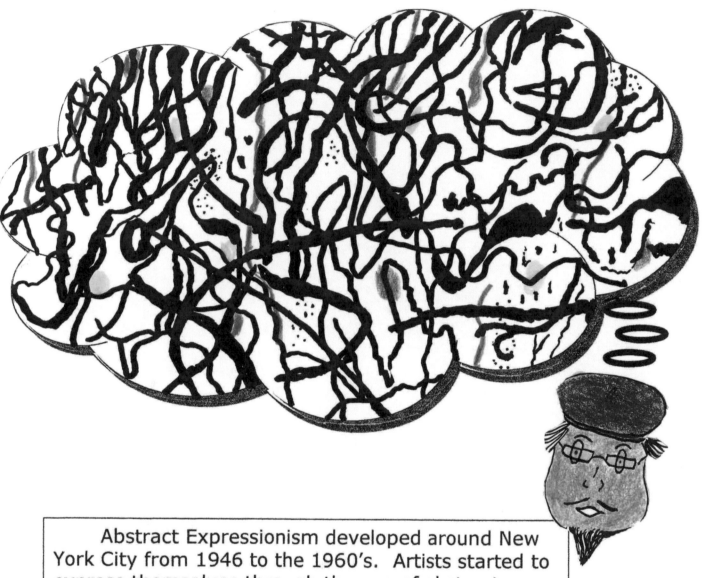

Abstract Expressionism developed around New York City from 1946 to the 1960's. Artists started to express themselves through the use of abstract forms and pure color on canvas. The artwork did not represent anything, nor could any object be identified in the painting. People started to consider how the artist might have felt, when he painted the painting (i.e. angry, sad, happy etc.).

Key Artists: Jackson Pollock

22

Op Art (optical art)

Op Art started to get popular around the 1960's. For the first time, artists were focused on creating optical illusions of motion and depth by means of simple and complex geometrical designs.

Key Artists: Victor Vasarely, Josef Albers , M.C. Escher, Bridget Riley, Richard Anuszkiewicz, François Morellet and Jesús-Rafael Soto.

23

Photorealism Art

Photorealism started around the late 1960s. Artists used cameras and photographs to gather information for their paintings. Many artists would take a slide and project the image onto a canvas and paint over the image. In Photorealism, time and movement are frozen and the painting appears similar to a photograph.

Key Artists: Richard Estes and Chuck Close.

Computer Generated Art

Today, we can find many computer programs that enable an artist to create unique two and three dimensional images. Computer operators can create mathematical models or use photographs to produce digital illustrations. Through the manipulation of a tablet or mouse, anyone can produce a digital illustration. What images or mystical worlds an artist can be imagine can now come alive on a screen.

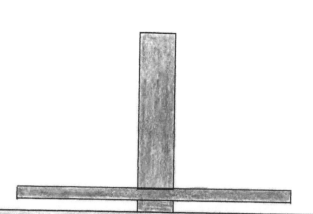

The Elements Of Design

are basic elements like color, line, shape, form, texture, and space which artists use to create a work of art.

28

The
Principles
Of
Design

are concepts like balance, movement, emphasis, rhythm, unity, patterns, and proportion, which artists use to organize the visual elements to create a work of art.

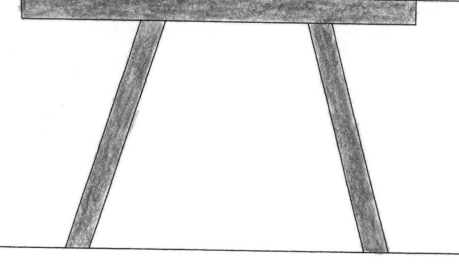

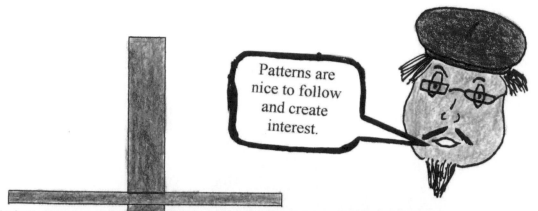

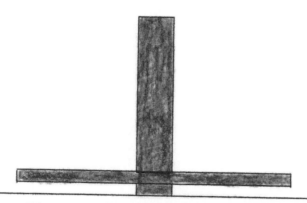

Examples of Art Materials

Tools:
Brushes
Airbrushes
Easels

Surfaces
Rocks
Wood
Glass
Canvas
Paper

Mediums
Color Pencils
Felt Tip Pens
Color Markers
Acrylic Paint
Oil Paint
Watercolour Paint
Oil Pastels
Chalk Pastels
Fabric Paint

An Individual Style of Art

One of the hardest things to do in art is to come up with ones own unique style. Trying to see or think of something that is different than anything that has come before. Greatness in art comes from this achievement. The Masters that started a style of painting had achieved this greatest. Today, there are many excellent artists that could paint in any style and their work demonstrates a high level of mastery, but to be true master they need to develop or contribute to the development of a new style. It is easy to copy a style but the true challenge is to create an original work of art in an original style.

Create Your Own Work of Art

IMAGINATION ON DISPLAY
FROM THE CAVES TO YOUR COMPUTER A NEW WAY SEEN THE WORLD

iUniverse books may be ordered through booksellers or by contacting:

iUniverse
1663 Liberty Drive
Bloomington, IN 47403
www.iuniverse.com
844-349-9409

Because of the dynamic nature of the Internet, any web addresses or links contained
in this book may have changed since publication and may no longer be valid. The views
expressed in this work are solely those of the author and do not necessarily reflect the
views of the publisher, and the publisher hereby disclaims any responsibility for them.

Any people depicted in stock imagery provided by Getty Images are models,
and such images are being used for illustrative purposes only.
Certain stock imagery © Getty Images.

ISBN: 978-1-6632-1805-6 (sc)
ISBN: 978-1-6632-1806-3 (e)

Library of Congress Control Number: 2021902267

Print information available on the last page.

iUniverse rev. date: 02/05/2021

Printed in the United States
by Baker & Taylor Publisher Services